FROM THE VERY BIG DESK OF. . .

"I can't believe it—a punk like me laying off an industry legend like you."

FROM THE VERY BIG DESK OF...

Business Cartoons by *New Yorker* Cartoonist

Charles Barsotti

Foreword by Andrew Tobias

BULFINCH PRESS

NEW YORK • BOSTON

To Ramoth

THE GREETING CARD AND THE BUSINESS LETTER

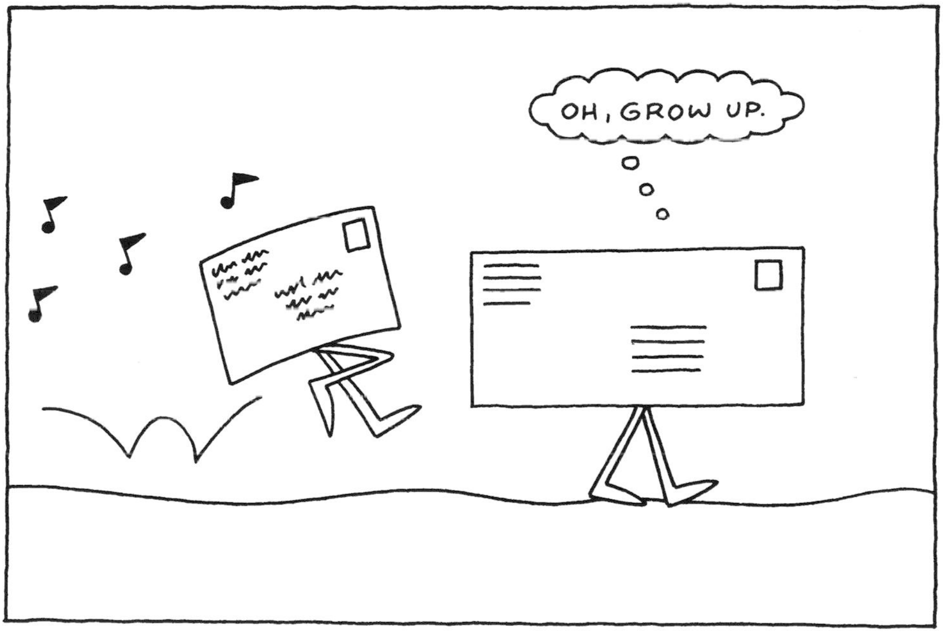

CBarsotti

I AM BESOTTED BY BARSOTTI. It began at least as far back as May 25, 1981—the date of the *New Yorker* issue in which appeared a drawing of a nebbishy, bespectacled old-style businessman with a mustache sitting at a plain desk with an intercom.

If he's a CEO, it's a small private company (and he thinks of himself as the boss, not the CEO). Or maybe he's the CFO of a somewhat bigger one. This is not a glamorous guy. His secretary has probably been with him for twenty years—and they are not having an affair.

He has his finger on the intercom. His secretary has just said, "Mike Wallace to see you, sir." He replies, "Terrific. Send him right in." The whole drawing is titled *Man with a Clear Conscience*.

I called the *New Yorker* and bought the original. Amazingly, no one from *60 Minutes* had beaten me to it. (Back then, it was almost a family affair—a relative few of us aficionados knew whom to call at the magazine, and for $300 or $400 the cartoon would be on its way. Today you go to www.cartoonbank.com and to galleries and the like—and for originals, expect to pay $1,500 or more.)

Man with a Clear Conscience hangs in my own office (not that I wouldn't get butterflies if Mike Wallace suddenly dropped in on *me*), and since then I have bought a dozen more—many from a Barsotti series I think of as "Geometry Man" (see, for example, pages 50 and 96 and, perhaps most wonderfully, 56. I have one, speaking of page 56, where the man peering down into the carton sees another man, to whom he says, "Who are you—and where the hell's my grapefruit?" (That may not be the precise caption; I have it hanging in Miami, closer to the grapefruit.)

And then there's *The Little Overnight Package That Could* with its little legs striving mightily. . . and the business letter saying to the greeting card, "Oh, grow up!". . . and the square man standing by his office door saying to the jagged, twisted man, "Mr. Wilson, I'm Dr. Bradshaw. Please come in."

And the executive made all of bubbles being eyed askance by a junior executive, to whom a coworker is saying, "Yes, but he's a vice president and you're not."

I have spent thousands of dollars on my Barsottis (and not a little on Mankoffs, Lorenzes, Chasts, Zieglers, and Wilsons, whose good artistic and comedic company at the *New Yorker* Charley Barsotti keeps). Yet the breadth of *your* collection, you lucky dog—held in your own hands right now and purchased for less than the cost of a single frame—far exceeds my own.

Enjoy!

Andrew Tobias, August 2005
New York

THE LITTLE OVERNIGHT PACKAGE THAT COULD

"Still, he's a vice-president and you're not."

FROM THE VERY BIG DESK OF. . .

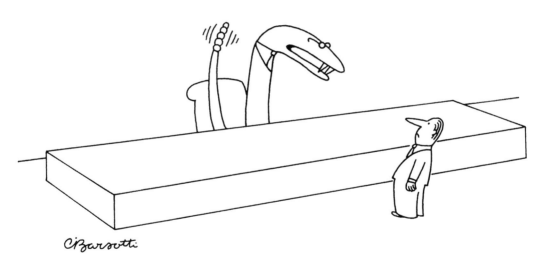

"You've been warned, Hoskins."

"Just tell him it's 'other people' as in 'other people's money.'"

"Ah, J. T.—just the man I was looking for."

"Did you hire a consultant? I didn't hire a consultant."

"Oh, I'm just riding out the cycle."

"There. Now it's all on paper. Feel better?"

"Look what I grew."

"Bad news, Gilchrist—somehow you've come to someone's attention."

TROUBLE

"Wentworth, could I take another look at that reorganization plan?"

"Sir, all the junior executives join me in thanking you for sending down the cookies."

"*The point is, Hutchens, a younger man could jump higher.*"

"Well, you certainly seem to have a lot to offer this company, and, of course, the truffles are a hell of a plus."

"Where'd you get that?"

"Help this poor wretch, Lord."

"Miss Richards, send in Rex the wonder dog, please."

"No, no, your job's not going out of the country to some foreign bastard. We're just firing you."

"I can't speak for everyone in the top one percent, but I'm fine."

"*I wonder, sir, if you would indulge me in a rather unusual request?*"

"So how many temps do you need?"

"No, sir, they don't come with the cubicle—you
have to order the cubicle separately."

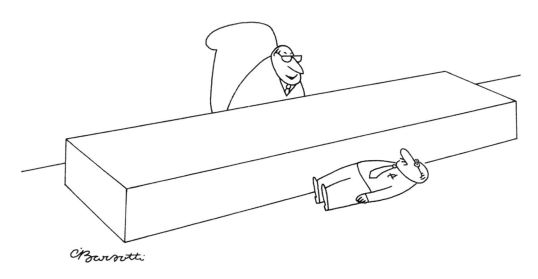

"Nothing personal, Wilson, I just wanted to see if I still had it."

"War, J.B., is the continuation of business by other means."

"Very good, Benson. That's what I want to see."

"As a company, and as individuals, we are without irony.
Will that bother you?"

"Miss Wexler, what are the prevailing winds?"

*"Mr. Hoffman? Ed Hoffman? Your office has been trying
to reach you, sir."*

"I work hard and I play hard."

"Then I wake up, the cheering has stopped, I have three kids, and I work in a cubicle."

"*Well, figuratively speaking, I've jumped a
few turnstiles in my day.*"

"No, I didn't. I never said there should be _no_ government regulation."

"Damn, I think I ate Plan B."

"I'm at the point where I find mixed signals reassuring."

"*Then it's agreed. We'll close our plants in Raleigh, Scranton, Kansas City,*
Toledo, Newark, Sacramento, Wheeling, and Houston.
Thank you, gentlemen. It was a very productive meeting."

"Then, gentlemen, it is the consensus of this meeting that we say nothing, do nothing, and hope it all blows over before our next meeting."

"Take my advice, Haskins, and keep your out-of-the-box ideas to yourself."

"You're amazing, Hargrave—fair weather or foul, good times or bad, boom or recession, you're always the same."

"*That's it. I'm taking the buyout.*"

"*We only hire temps, and you have a look of permanence about you.*"

"I don't want stock options. I want you to pay your tab."

"We still haven't worked out all the kinks in the capitalist system, have we, J.B.?"

"Oh, that's a break. His job description is right on top."

"I wouldn't say anything, Elliot, but your mood is
affecting everyone in the office."

"Hey everybody, Quigley is practicing his perp walk."

"That was Swanson, sir. He wasn't on the list, but I'll add him."

"*The board of directors has given me new powers.*"

"Oh, darn, now I've ceded the moral high ground."

"Look, it's no problem. Just tell me which Mr. Kessler
you had an appointment with."

"Let it go. I was thinking of taking early retirement anyway."

"*Sorry, Elliott, but everything in this file is to be put on microfilm.*"

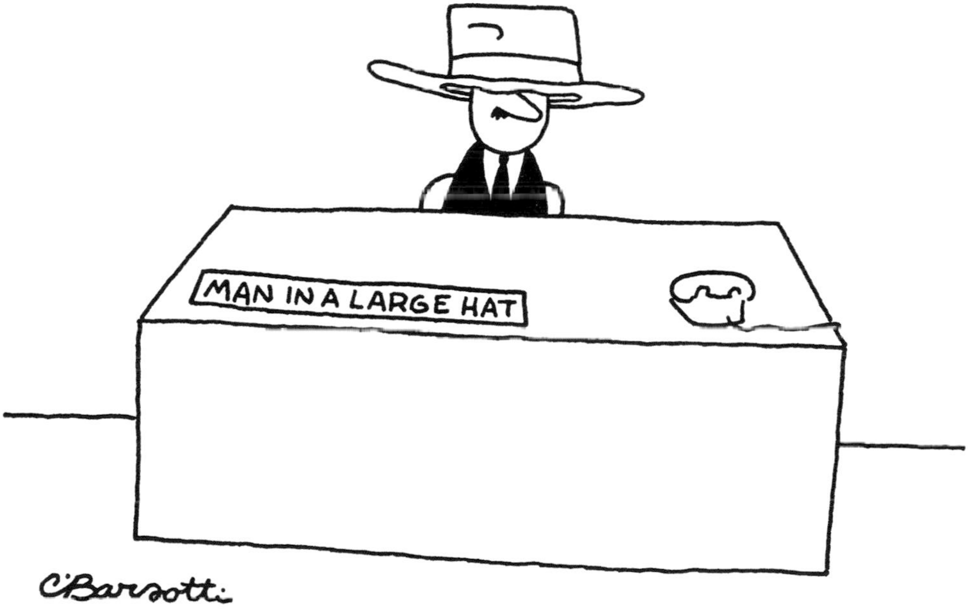
MAN IN A LARGE HAT
CBarsotti

"Have you ever considered another line of work?"

"'I yam what I yam an' tha's all I yam!'
What the hell kind of résumé is that?"

"What the hell? We could use an idiot."

"Sorry, you're overqualified."

"Gosh, I wish somebody would tell <u>me</u> to take early retirement."

"*And when the time comes the company will put you to sleep at its own expense.*"

"Nonsense, Braddock, you do have a life."

"Mr. Wilson? I'm Dr. Bradshaw. Please come in."

"I need another week."

"Any other objections?"

"*Still, Edgar, you were loyal longer than most, and
I'd like to thank you for that.*"

"I'd rather drown."

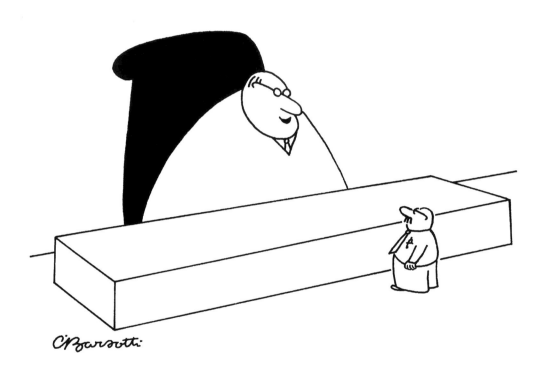

"I won't of course, Hollingsworth, but I could have you killed."

"*I plead guilty, Your Honor, but only in a nice, white-collar sort of way.*"

"By God, you're not a man who's afraid to fail."

"*Is it my fault he guessed the wrong hand?*"

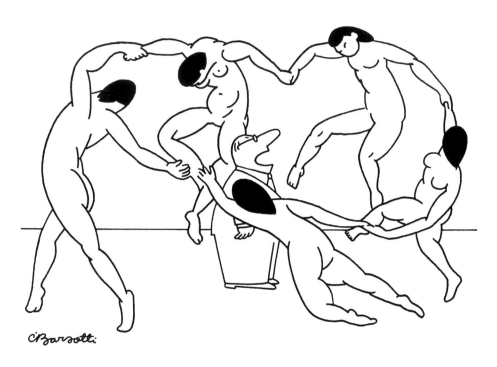

"*Do I have to remind you people that we're facing a <u>hostile</u> takeover?*"

"Just a few more pages, Hansen, and we'll take a short break."

"Yes, sir, morale is fine."

*"And yet, as we look at our lives, can't many of us say, 'My cubicle
is too small'?"*

"It's simple enough, Langdon, but I'll explain again. To help pay off
the debt that we incurred when we bought this company,
we've sold some of you into slavery."

"You're fired, Pembroke. We're turning the office into a smoke-free environment."

"Benign so far."

"What I'll miss most is his indefatigable optimism."

"*Thank you. We're all refreshed and challenged by your unique point of view. Now, we have many serious matters to discuss today, so I suggest we stick with our agreed-upon agenda.*"

"Good, we're all agreed. I like it when we're all agreed."

"Let Halliburton clean it up."

"Don't say it never trickled."

"Good grief, Bradbury! How long have you been working at home?"

"Surely you can't hold me responsible for what others might say."

"Would you like a little phone sex while you hold?"

"*Well, make yourself useful while you're steeping.*"

"Throw in some marinara sauce and you've got a deal."

"OK, OK, Wilkins, on behalf of all alpha males I apologize."

"*Damn straight, if the food chain ain't broke, don't fix it.*"

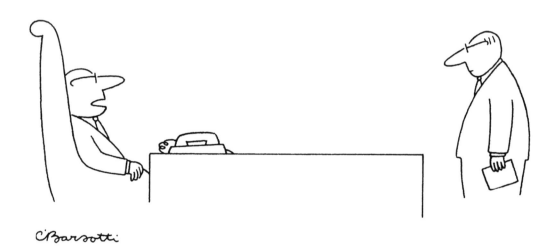

"Send Williamson a signal. Tell him he's fired."

"*Henceforth, Illingworth, I will expect you to have your act together before you arrive at the office.*"

"*Oh, I had some elevator trouble in the morning, but overall it was a pretty good day.*"

"As CEO, I try to look at the big picture, while J.G., as president, sees to the day-to-day operations."

"Do you have to do that now?"

Acknowledgments

Thanks to Michael Sand, Alex Isley, and my friends at
The Cartoon Bank. I am hugely grateful to Martha Kaplan for
her friendship and faith-based support. And finally I'd like to
take back almost everything I've said about *New Yorker* cartoon
editors Lee Lorenz and Bob Mankoff.

Bulfinch Press

Time Warner Book Group
1271 Avenue of the Americas, New York, NY 10020
Visit our Web site at www.bulfinchpress.com

First Edition: May 2006

ISBN-10: 0-8212-5793-5
ISBN-13: 978-0-8212-5793-7
Library of Congress Control Number: 2005933843

For information regarding sales to corporations, organizations, mail-order catalogs, premiums, and other non-book retailers and wholesalers, contact:

Special Markets Department
Time Warner Book Group
1271 Ave. of the Americas, 12th Floor
New York, NY 10020-1393
Tel: 1-800-222-6747

Cartoon production assistance provided by The Cartoon Bank, a *New Yorker* Magazine company

Book design by Gail Doobinin

PRINTED IN SINGAPORE

FROM THE VERY BIG DESK OF...

C. Barsotti